DOLPHINS

by Scott Ingram

Consultant: Jenny Montague
Assistant Curator of Marine Mammals
New England Aquarium
Boston, MA

BEARPORT
PUBLISHING COMPANY, INC.

New York, New York

Credits

Cover (center), © Jeffrey L. Rotman/CORBIS; Cover (background), The Cover Story/CORBIS; Title Page, © Jeffrey L. Rotman/CORBIS; 4–5, Marine Animal Productions, Gulfport, MS; 6, Xavier Safont/Imagequestmarine.com; 7, Courtesy of The Monkey Mia Research Foundation, photo by Amanda Coakes; 8, Michael S. Nolan/SeaPics.com; 9, Doug Perrine/SeaPics.com; 10, Doug Perrine/SeaPics.com; 12, Tim Hellier/Imagequestmarine.com; 13–15, EarthTrust, Honolulu; 16, Jeff Jaskolski/SeaPics.com; 17, © Bob Krist/CORBIS; 18–19, The Dolphin Institute, Honolulu, HI, www.dolphin-institute.org; 20, Michael S. Nolan/SeaPics.com; 21, Daniel McCulloch/SeaPics.com; 22, Dave Herring; 23, Doug Perrine/SeaPics.com; 24(map), Dave Herring; 24, Courtesy of Richard B. Mieremet, NOAA's Ark Collection; 25 (top right), Michael S. Nolan/SeaPics.com; 25 (top left), Gregory Ochocki/SeaPics.com; 25 (bottom), Ingrid Visser/SeaPics.com; 26, Werner Foreman/Art Resource; 27, Alexis Rosenfeld/Photo Researchers, Inc.; 28, Doug Perrine/SeaPics.com; 29, The Dolphin Institute, Honolulu, HI, www.dolphin-institute.org.

Design and production by Dawn Beard Creative and Octavo Design and Production, Inc.

Special thanks to:
The Dolphin Institute, 420 Ward Ave., Suite 212,
Honolulu, HI 96814; 808-593-2211; www.dolphin-institute.org;
pack@ dolphin-institute.org

Marine Life Oceanarium, Gulfport, MS

Library of Congress Cataloging-in-Publication Data

Ingram, Scott.
Dolphins / by Scott Ingram.
p. cm.—(Smart animals!)
Includes bibliographical references and index.
ISBN 1-59716-161-6 (library binding)—ISBN 1-59716-187-X (pbk.)
1. Dolphins—Juvenile literature. 2. Animal intelligence—Juvenile literature. I. Title. II. Series.

QL737.C432I54 2006
599.53—dc22

2005026825

For more information, write to Bearport Publishing Company, Inc., 101 Fifth Avenue, Suite 6R, New York, New York 10003. Printed in the United States of America.

1 2 3 4 5 6 7 8 9 10

Contents

Planning Ahead

Kelly searched the pool. If she found any paper, she would get a fish. For a dolphin like Kelly, it was the perfect **reward**.

Trainers had taught Kelly to bring them **litter** that fell in the water. On days when there was no trash, she could not get extra fish. So Kelly learned to plan ahead.

▲ **Kelly is a bottlenose dolphin from the Marine Life Oceanarium in Gulfport, Mississippi.**

Kelly hid the pieces of paper she found. She saved them under a rock. The next time trainers asked her to search for litter, Kelly would be ready. She wouldn't even have to search the pool. Scientists say that planning ahead is a sign of a smart animal.

▲ **Kelly jumps 15 feet (5 m) in the air to take a fish from her trainer's mouth.**

Some scientists believe that dolphins are one of the smartest animals in the world. Gorillas, chimpanzees, parrots, and elephants are also very smart.

Using Tools

Kelly used her **beak** to pick up the litter she found. Dolphins also use their beaks to catch fish. Hunting in the ocean, however, can be dangerous. Some fish have stingers and sharp fins. They can hurt the beaks of dolphins. How do some dolphins solve this problem?

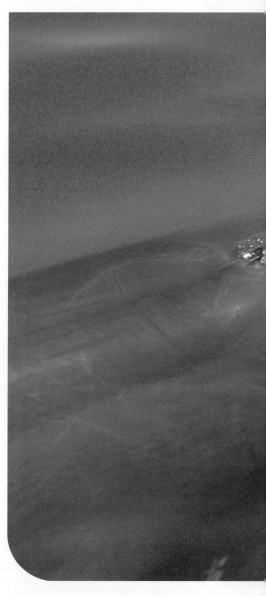

▲ **Stonefish have sharp spines that can harm dolphins hunting for food on the rocky ocean floor.**

Dolphins use the sharp fins of dead fish as a **tool** to poke at eels hiding between rocks.

The dolphins put soft **sponges** on their beaks. They use the sponges as a tool to protect themselves from getting stung or cut by fish. Now the dolphins can hunt without getting hurt. Using tools to solve problems is another way animals show they are **intelligent**.

▲ **Some dolphins use sponges to protect their beaks.**

Dolphins Are Not Fish

Dolphins live in water, but they are not fish. Dolphins are **mammals**. Humans, monkeys, cats, and dogs are also examples of mammals.

Most fish lay eggs. Almost all mammals, however, give birth to live young. The newborns drink milk from their mothers. Mother dolphins **nurse** their babies, called calves, for more than a year.

▲ **Atlantic spotted dolphin nursing her calf**

All mammals use lungs to breathe air. Most take in air through their noses and mouths. Dolphins, however, use the **blowhole** on top of their heads. They come up to the water's surface to get air. When they go back down, they close the blowhole to keep water from getting in their lungs.

◄ **Dolphin blowhole**

Dolphin **flippers** have bones that look like long fingers.

Working Together

Dolphins often work in groups, called **pods**, to catch fish. Working together is a smart way to feed everyone.

First, the dolphins swim circles around a **school** of fish. The dolphins keep swimming in tighter circles. They force the fish into a small area. Soon the fish are trapped.

Then the dolphins take turns swimming through the school. They catch fish as they swim. By working together, everyone gets a chance to eat.

◄ **A pod of dolphins trapping a school of fish**

Sometimes a pod helps a sick dolphin that may not be able to swim to the surface to breathe. Dolphins in the pod take turns holding up the sick dolphin so that he can get air.

It's Smart to Play

While dolphins work together to help one another, they also like to play. Scientists say playing is a sign of a smart animal.

Some dolphins chase each other or play catch with pieces of seaweed. They also surf on the waves made by boats.

▲ **Dolphins play by racing ahead of boats.**

Scientists saw Tinkerbell and Maui (MOU-ee), two baby dolphins, making their own toys. The babies blew air from their blowholes to make bubble rings. Then the dolphins played with the air rings by moving them around or biting them. They even bounced the rings off the wall of their pool.

◀ **A baby dolphin playing with a bubble ring**

Dolphins sometimes play with other animals. They may pull feathers from a seabird's tail. They sometimes play catch using fish.

Keola Sees Himself

Keola (key-OH-lah) was a bottlenose dolphin who lived at Sea Life Park in Hawaii. One day, scientists tried an **experiment** to see how smart he was. They wanted to see if Keola could look in a mirror and understand that he was seeing himself.

▲ **Scientists studying dolphins**

First, the scientists put a mirror under water. Then they made a mark on Keola's body. The dolphin could only see the mark when he looked in the mirror.

What happened? When Keola swam to the mirror, he positioned his body so that he could see where the mark had been made. Keola understood he was looking at himself in the mirror.

▲ **Keola with mark on the side of his body**

Besides dolphins, chimpanzees are one of the few animals that recognize themselves in mirrors.

Understanding Humans

Scientists have studied many dolphins, like Keola, to find out if humans can **communicate** with them. Some dolphin trainers have developed a sign language that dolphins can understand.

▲ **This trainer and child use hand signals to tell a dolphin to show his teeth.**

The trainer makes a signal with her hand. Each signal is like a word. It tells the dolphin what to do. For example, one signal means "jump out of the water."

Dolphins have been taught to understand many different hand signals. They've learned to fetch toys, leap over objects, and jump through the air.

Making Their Own Decisions

Researchers at The Dolphin Institute in Hawaii have taught two dolphins to decide on their own what action to perform together. First, a trainer makes a hand signal that tells Phoenix (FEE-niks) and Akeakamai (uh-KAY-UH-kam-eye) to choose any action. Then the trainer quickly follows with a second signal that means "do it together." No one knows exactly what the dolphins will perform.

▲ **Phoenix and Akeakamai**

The two dolphins dive down. The trainers wait to see what they will do. This time, they have decided to leap up out of the water together. The dolphins understood the trainer's signals, and each other.

▲ Here, Phoenix and Akeakamai have chosen to turn upside down and lift up their tails together.

Akeakamai understands the meaning of hand signals for objects and actions, even when they occur in a row. For example, "take the hoop to the surfboard" or "take the surfboard to the hoop." She knows that the same signs placed in different orders tell her to do different things.

Making Sounds

To communicate with dolphins, people use hand signals. Dolphins, however, use sounds to communicate with one another.

Dolphins make whistle-like sounds to **identify** themselves. It's a way to tell the other members of the group who they are. Each dolphin's whistle is like his or her name.

A mother will whistle for days after her baby is born. The baby can then recognize her mother's sound.

▲ **Mother dolphin and calf**

Dolphins also use sounds to express feelings. When dolphins are upset, they may open their mouths and then slam them closed. This sound is called a "jaw pop."

Dolphins use more than their blowholes and jaws to make sounds. They also slap the water with their tails or flippers to communicate with other animals.

◄ **When dolphins play, they may make squeaking sounds.**

Seeing with Ears

Dolphins make clicking sounds to help them find fish and stay away from dangerous animals, such as sharks. The dolphins aim the clicks with the large, rounded part of their head, called the **melon**. The clicks bounce off objects and return to the dolphin. This bounce is called an **echo**.

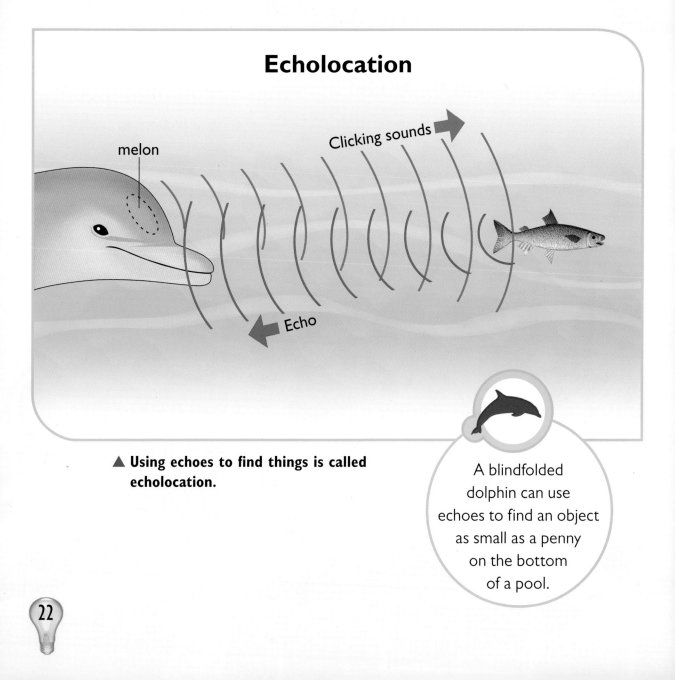

Echolocation

melon

Clicking sounds

Echo

▲ **Using echoes to find things is called echolocation.**

A blindfolded dolphin can use echoes to find an object as small as a penny on the bottom of a pool.

Dolphins can tell the size, shape, and distance of an object by listening to the echoes. They use the clicks to find food that is too far away to see with their eyes. Dolphins also use echoes to find fish that are buried under sand.

▲ **This dolphin is hunting for fish hidden in the sand.**

Dolphins Live in Many Places

Dolphins are divided into **species**, such as the bottlenose dolphin and the spinner dolphin. There are more than 30 different dolphin species. This map shows the places where bottlenose dolphins live.

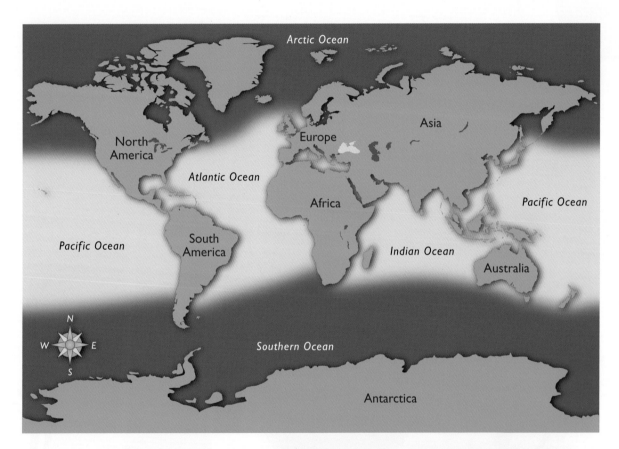

Range of the bottlenose dolphin

Dolphins live in every ocean of the world. Five dolphin species live in rivers. They are named after the rivers where they live, such as the Amazon River dolphin.

▲ **Amazon River dolphin**

▲ **Spinner dolphin**

The orca, or killer whale, is the largest member of the dolphin family.

▲ **Orca**

25

Fascinating Animals

Whether playing in the waves, hunting for fish, or using tools, dolphins have **fascinated** humans for thousands of years. People have put their pictures on coins, pottery, statues, and even cave walls.

In ancient Greece, a person who killed a dolphin could be punished with death.

▲ **A soldier riding a dolphin on a Greek vase that is over 2,000 years old**

People always seemed to know there was something special about dolphins. Now scientists are finding out that these clever animals may be smarter than we ever thought.

Just the Facts

Bottlenose Dolphin

Weight	330–775 pounds (150–352 kg)
Length	6–13 feet (2–4 m)
Life Span	25–30 years, though some may live to 50 years
Average Speed	3–6 miles per hour (5–10 kph), but they can reach speeds of 21 miles per hour (34 kph)
Food	mainly fish and squid
Habitat	mostly warm and tropical water in both the Pacific and Atlantic oceans
Predators	large shark species, such as tiger sharks, dusky sharks, and bull sharks

More Smart Dolphins

At The Dolphin Institute, Elele (ee-LAY-lay) learned that different hand signals from a trainer can stand for nine different parts of her body. Some of these parts are the mouth, melon, side, belly, and tail. Trainers used the signs to ask Elele to use a body part in different ways. For example, touching a ball with her tail, waving her tail in the air, or touching a surfboard with her belly.

Dolphins are great at copying one another's actions. Yet they can also be taught to copy people's movements. If a human twirls around, so does the dolphin. Dolphins can even copy movements when they don't have the same body parts as people. If a person raises her leg, the dolphin raises her tail.

◀ **Dolphins can copy human movements.**

Glossary

beak (BEEK) for animals such as dolphins and birds, the hard, horn-shaped part of their mouths

blowhole (BLOH-hohl) the opening at the top of a dolphin's head that allows the animal to get air

communicate (kuh-MYOO-nuh-kate) to pass on facts, ideas, thoughts, or feelings

echo (EK-oh) a sound that bounces off an object and returns to the place where it came from

experiment (ek-SPER-uh-ment) a scientific test set up to find the answer to a question

fascinated (FASS-uh-*nay*-tid) held one's attention

flippers (FLIP-urz) fins on either side of a dolphin that are used to steer or guide the body

identify (eye-DEN-tuh-*fye*) to tell who someone is or what something is

intelligent (in-TEL-uh-juhnt) smart

litter (LIT-ur) trash

mammals (MAM-uhlz) animals that are warm-blooded, nurse their young with milk, and have hair or fur on their skin

melon (MEL-uhn) the large, rounded area in the front of a dolphin's head that aims clicking sounds toward objects under water

nurse (NURSS) to feed a young animal milk that comes from the baby's mother

pods (PODZ) groups of dolphins that live together

reward (ri-WORD) what a person or animal gets for doing something useful or good

school (SKOOL) a group of the same kind of fish or other sea animals that are swimming together

species (SPEE-sheez) groups that animals are divided into, according to similar characteristics; members of the same species can have offspring

sponges (SPUHNJ-iz) simple sea animals that have many holes through which water flows

tool (TOOL) an object that is used to help do a job

trainers (TRAY-nurz) people who teach animals or other people to do something

Bibliography

Cerullo, Mary M. *Dolphins: What They Can Teach Us.* New York: Dutton Children's Books (1999).

Dudzinski, Kathleen. *Meeting Dolphins: My Adventures in the Sea.* Washington, D.C.: National Geographic Society (2000).

Hirschmann, Kris. *Dolphins: Creatures of the Sea.* San Diego, CA: KidHaven Press (2003).

Read More

Crisp, Marty. *Everything Dolphin.* Minnetonka, MN: Northword Press (2004).

Grover, Wayne. *Dolphin Adventure: A True Story.* New York: HarperTrophy (2000).

Osborne, Mary Pope, and Natalie Pope Boyce. *Dolphins and Sharks.* New York: Random House (2003).

Vogel, Julia. *Dolphins (Our Wild World).* Minnetonka, MN: Northword Press (2001).

Learn More Online

Visit these Web sites to learn more about dolphins:

www.nationalgeographic.com/kids/creature_feature/0108/dolphins.html

www.seaworld.org/animal-info/info-books/bottlenose/index.htm

Index

About the Author

Scott Ingram has written more than 50 books for young people. He lives in Connecticut, near a marine life aquarium that is home to several dolphin species.